For Tage, Savva, Kaia, and Gregor-David
K. H.

For Sam, James, and Beatrice
P. H.

Text copyright © 2006 by Kathy Henderson
Illustrations copyright © 2006 by Paul Howard

First U.S. edition 2006

Library of Congress Cataloging-in-Publication Data is available.

Library of Congress Catalog Card Number 2005050792

ISBN-13: 978-0-7636-2745-4
ISBN-10: 0-7636-2745-3

1 2 3 4 5 6 7 8 9 10

Printed in China

This book was typeset in FC Contemporary Brush.
The illustrations were done in pencil and watercolor.

Candlewick Press
2067 Massachusetts Avenue
Cambridge, Massachusetts 02140

visit us at www.candlewick.com

LOOK
AT
YOU!

A Baby Body Book

KATHY HENDERSON illustrated by PAUL HOWARD

CANDLEWICK PRESS
CAMBRIDGE, MASSACHUSETTS

Fingers and toes wiggle.

Eyes, nose, and mouth giggle.

Arms wave, legs kick . . .

bottoms squirm . . .
and tummies tickle.

Clothes on.

Where's the baby gone?

There
he is!

Clothes off!

Where are the baby's toes?

There they are!

Lie
roll
sit
wobble.

Rock

crawl

pull

wobble.

Stand

wobble.

Sway

wobble.

Bump!

Step

walk

toddle!

What can you
see?

Something
to eat.

What can you
hear?

A song
in the
air.

And how does it feel?

Warm and squelchy, scratchy, rough, sticky, squishy . . .

Time for a bath!

Float   soap

splash

wash

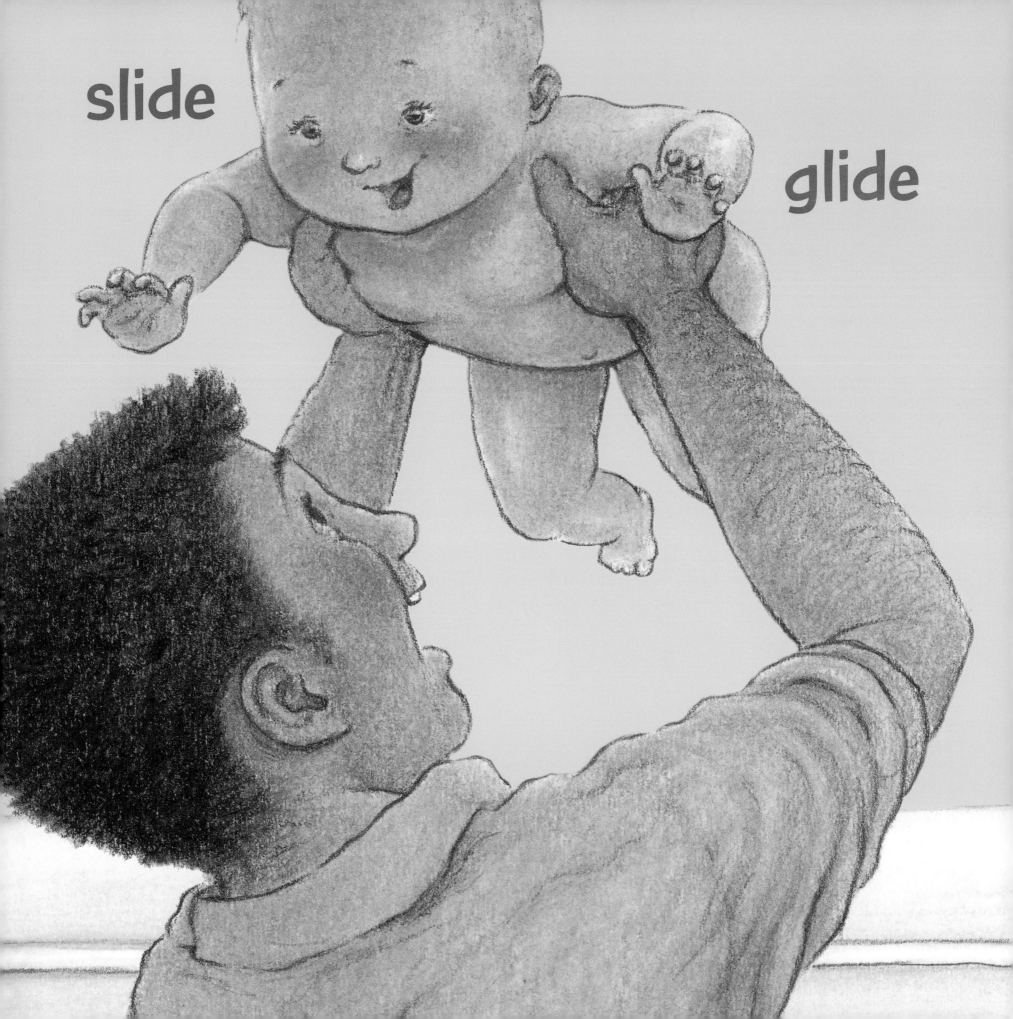

cuddle

brush.

Clip, snip, some things grow quick.

Hey ho, others grow slow!

Funny thing, hair . . .
You can brush it this way,
you can brush it that,
wash it, dry it, tie it up,
and squash it flat.

I feel . . .

good

bad

happy

sad

bold

shy
(I don't know why).

I feel
lonely.

I feel
fine.

A-a-a-chooo!

Wow, what a body can do!

Yawn! Hic!

Plenty of tricks.

Whoops! . . .
Phew! . . .

Wow, what a body can do!

Sigh, flop, snuggle down,
curl up in a heap.

The story's done, this body's tired,
and now it's going to sleep.